Stories I've Told!

A Collection of Tellable Tales

Robert Djed Snead

MoonWater Products

First Edition

Published by:
MoonWater Products
63 Roycroft Drive
Rochester, New York 14621

MOON
WATER
PRODUCTS

MoonWater Products
http//:djedsnead.webs.com

Manufactured and printed in the U.S.A.

Introduction

When I was growing up we were not allowed to say the word "lie." We had to say "storying.." ...but storytelling is everything but "lying."

Wonderful, insightful truths can be conveyed by a tale well told. Understanding and power, wisdom beyond words, and freedom can be shared from teller to listeners, and back to teller...

My prayer is that you are blessed by reading the stories in this book, and then blessed again in sharing them with others....

djed

Dedication

This book is dedicated to my sons- Aaron, Adam, Amon and Alijah (The A-team). I am in awe of each of you....

dad
April 2014

CONTENTS

Original Stories

Retold Stories

Aesop Retold

ORIGINAL STORIES

AZIZA

Once upon a time in Hausa land, in northern Nigeria, there lived a young man. The young man and his wife were extremely happy because they had just found out that they were going to become parents for the first time. All of the parents in their village loved and cherished their children.

When the baby was born it was a girl! And as was the age-old custom in the village the young man and his wife waited 7 days before naming the child.

On the seventh day the whole village gathered in the young man's compound. There was singing and there was dancing. There was food and there was drink.

At the appropriate time the young man stood, and there was silence.

Facing the North, and in a loud, clear voice, the young man said, "*Aziza!*" He turned to the East and said, "*Aziza!*" He turned to the South and said, "*Aziza!*" He turned to the West and said, "*Aziza!*"

It was thus that the young man let the four Winds and the whole world know the newborn's name would be Aziza. Now Aziza means "beautiful."

When the people in the village saw the baby they said, "*Yes*, this is a beautiful baby!" Some of the people in the village even said that this was the most beautiful baby ever born in the village.

The newborn's head was shaved and special markings were put on her head to identify her as a member of the village.

And as Aziza grew not only was she beautiful in face and in form, but she also had a pleasing personality. She never seemed to have a bad day. Aziza carried her weather within. All of the children and the adults in the village loved to spend time with her.

And as Aziza grew her mother would take her into the forest and show her the roots and the herbs: which ones were good for cooking, and which ones were not. Her mother would show her the plants and flowers: which ones were good for healing, and which ones were not.

And as Aziza grew the people in the village would say, "What beautiful eyes you have, Aziza!" "What a wonderful smile you have Aziza!" "What a pleasing personality you have Aziza!"

Time come and time go, and Aziza became a young maiden.

All of the young men from her village and the surrounding villages came to ask Aziza's father for her hand in marriage.

It was the custom in the village to bring a gift to the maiden's father you came courting.

Aziza's father was in no hurry for the gifts to end. When the young men would ask him for his decision he would respond, "Patience, patience! Soon I will make my decision. Patience...."

One day Aziza was in the family compound pounding millet. Into the compound fluttered a beautiful butterfly. It was yellow. It was red. It was orange. It was gold.

Aziza thought to herself, "What a wonderful gift this would make for my mother".

Aziza tried to catch the butterfly but every time she came close to catching the butterfly it would flutter away. Each time Aziza tried to catch the butterfly it would flutter away.

The butterfly left the compound and went deep into the forest next to Aziza's village. Aziza followed.

The butterfly landed on a stone and Aziza crept up on it. She was getting ready to catch the butterfly when magically the butterfly transformed itself into a handsome, well-dressed young man.

Aziza was both surprised and frightened, but she acted as if she was neither.

"My name is Iblis," the young man said, "and I have come for your hand in marriage, Aziza. I have come from far away." Iblis pointed toward the sky.

He said, "My mother is the Moon and my father is the Wind and I must have your hand in marriage and you must come and live with me in the sky."

Aziza responded, "I am humbled that someone as noble and beautiful as you would consider me worthy to be your bride. But I cannot make the decision as to whom I shall marry. Only my father can decide who can have my hand in marriage."

Aziza had just gotten these words out of her mouth when Iblis became angry with her and began screaming and yelling at her.

"You must marry me Aziza and come and live with me in the sky! If you refuse to marry me I will have my father destroy your village and kill all of the people in your village! I will come back tomorrow for your answer!"

Iblis transformed himself back into the beautiful butterfly and fluttered away.

As Aziza made her way back to her village her mind was full of thoughts.

She thought, "How could something be so beautiful and be so bad?"

She thought, "I do not want to marry Iblis and go and live with him in the sky"

She thought, "But I do not want Iblis to have his father destroy my village and kill all of the people in my village."

All through the night Aziza thought, and she thought, and she thought and she thought! And with the rising sun Aziza had came up with a plan that she hoped would save both herself and her village.

Later that day Aziza was sitting in the family compound pounding millet. Into the compound fluttered the beautiful butterfly. It was red. It was orange. It was yellow. It was gold.

Iblis flew over to Aziza and said, "Follow me Aziza!"

Aziza followed Iblis and the butterfly went back into the forest and landed on the same stone as the day before.

—
13

Iblis transformed himself back into the handsome young man.

"Very well then, Aziza, what did your father say?" Iblis asked.

Aziza responded, "I did not ask my father. You see, there is a custom in my village that if you want my hand in marriage you must bring my father a gift."

Iblis became angry again and began to threaten and yell at Aziza but she stood quietly and waited for him to become quiet again.

"Very well then Aziza, what is it that your father likes?" Iblis asked annoyed.

"Sweets! My father loves sweets," Aziza replied. "Fine, I will get him some honey and that shall be the end of it," Iblis stated. Aziza smiled and shook her head. "Almost all of the men who have asked for my hand in marriage have brought my father honey. He has had his fill of honey. You must bring him a sweetness that he has never tasted before."

Aziza pointed at a red flower that she

was standing next to. "Bring my father the sweetness from this flower and then I am sure he will give you my hand in marriage."

Iblis walked over to where Aziza was standing. "But Aziza how can I get the sweetness from this flower?" Iblis asked, getting irritated again.

"Become the beautiful butterfly and it will be easy," Aziza replied softly.

And with that Iblis transformed himself back into the beautiful butterfly and then he could smell the sweetness, the pungency of the flower.

Iblis landed on the leaves of the flower and began to gather the nectar from the flower.

Then suddenly: Whap! Without warning the leaves of the flower enclosed Iblis and the more he struggled the tighter the leaves of the Venus's fly-trap became. The more he struggled the tighter the leaves became.

From inside the flower Aziza heard, *"Aziza!!! You tricked me!...."* Then there was silence.

Aziza waited a full 3 hours to make sure that Iblis did not escape.

As she made her way back to her village her mind was full of thoughts. .

She thought, "How could something be so beautiful and be so bad?"

She thought, "I am glad now that when my mother was teaching me about the roots and the herbs, the flowers and the plants I listened."

She thought, "I, Aziza, one day, when I am married, will tell my children, how I, Aziza, saved both myself and my village from a beautiful butterfly name Iblis."

OBADIAH

Once upon a time in the days of King Herod there lived a man named Obadiah. Obadiah lived in the province of Galilee near the border with Samaria.

Obadiah was doing all right for himself. He was a trader in salt and business was good. He had a large and healthy family, and he drove a two-year-old chariot. Obadiah was doing all right!

One day Obadiah was vacationing at the Jordan River when he noticed a crowd gathering around a strange looking fellow dressed in a camel hair suit.

When Obadiah asked someone who this fellow was he was told "John the Baptist." Well Obadiah knew the dude didn't have good sense because it was 90 degrees in the shade and John had to be burning up in that hot camel's hair suit!

Obadiah was checking out John and trying to figure out where he might be from when another fellow (who Obadiah could tell from his clothes was from Galilee like him) came up to John and was baptized.

Right after this Galilean fellow got baptized he took off running like the devil was behind! Obadiah just shook his head and he wondered what this world was coming to.

About two months after this Obadiah started hearing about that same Galilean fellow he had seen running off from the Jordan that day. Come to find out his name was Jesus. Now Jesus had gotten together a group of followers (he called them his disciples), and that was when things really started to pick up for Jesus.

Obadiah heard that Jesus had preached his trial sermon at the synagogue at Capernaum and it had went so well that Jesus was tearing up synagogues all throughout Galilee. He heard that Jesus was preaching with authority.

Now Obadiah wasn't there but he heard that Jesus was casting out demons; Obadiah heard that Jesus had healed a paralyzed man, and another man with a withered hand!

Out of all the things that Obadiah had heard about this Jesus the one he found the most difficult to believe was that Jesus had cured a man of *leprosy*!

Now leprosy wasn't no joke! If Jesus had came up with some kind of cure for leprosy Obadiah wanted to have a little talk with Jesus himself about a little business proposition.

The biggest problem was now that Jesus was getting to be such a big star people started coming out in droves to see what would Jesus do next.

Everywhere that Jesus went the crowds were sure to go. Everywhere that Jesus went the crowds were sure to go!

Nobody wanted to miss Jesus' next miracle, or miss Jesus' next sermon, or miss his next parable.

Obadiah made up his mind that he was going to check this Jesus dude out for himself. Obadiah heard that Jesus was on vacation and had sent out his disciples 2 by 2 to spread the word about where he would be appearing next.

Obadiah's cousin Naamon, who lived just south of Nazareth, had allowed a couple of the disciples to stay with him when they passed through his village.

Naamon told Obadiah that the disciples didn't look like they were doing all that well financially. Naamon told Obadiah that the disciples told him that Jesus told them not to take any food or money with them in their travels; Naamon said they said that Jesus said they should take one suit of clothes, their walking stick, and to wear sandals.

Now when Naamon first took the disciples in he thought it was just going to be overnight. Naamon told Obadiah that those rascals stayed with him the whole week they visited in his village. And all they did was *talk, talk, talk* about some "New Kingdom" at hand!

Naamon told Obadiah that he listened to them boys but to him they sounded confused and needed to get a real job! Naamon told Obadiah the disciples told him that Jesus told them that if they came to a village that wouldn't put them up for a while they should shake the dust from their sandals at the village as a testimony against them. Like that was going to hurt the village's feelings or something! Naamon told Obadiah that those boys were really confused!

Obadiah had to take care of some business at King Herod's palace (he was contesting his income tax return from the previous year) and all he heard the civil servants and big shots talking about was Jesus this and Jesus that!

Now Obadiah said to himself if everybody here knew about Jesus he knew King Herod must have heard about him too! Now this was the same King Herod who had had John the Baptist beheaded for his wife Herodias' daughter. If the king knew your name you know you had made it.

Jesus had come a long way from being a carpenter in Nazareth. Jesus was a star in the ghetto. Jesus had a rep in the hood.

Obadiah really made up his mind that he had to check this Jesus out for himself now.

Obadiah heard that Jesus and his disciples were going to an "out-of-the-way-place." Well everybody knew what that meant so as the word spread about Jesus and the disciples going to the "out-of-the-way-place" people started heading there to get a good seat.

Everywhere that Jesus went the crowds were sure to go.....

Obadiah got his traveling bag, his walking stick, and put on an extra robe and went to that "out-of-the-way-place."

When Obadiah got there there must have been 5,000 men there, not counting the women and children. Jesus and his disciples were just getting off the boat and a hush fell over the crowd.

Obadiah looked around and he could tell from the different clothes and complexions that some of the people were from as far away as Idumea and Bashan, some from Phoenicia and Samaria, and some were from Judea and Galilee.

Then Jesus began to talk and it was the

sound of a soothing breeze. Jesus told a couple of jokes and the crowd burst out laughing, all together. Obadiah caught himself laughing, and listening, with the crowd. Jesus continued to talk, his voice rising and falling with the points he was making.

Sometimes he sounded angry, sometimes mocking, sometimes so serious. Jesus used parables to make some of his points crystal clear.

Obadiah felt himself caught up in the moment. Obadiah felt all 5,000 men, not counting women and children, as one; one heart, one mind, one voice. Obadiah was lifted up.

It was getting late before Obadiah realized it. Nobody had left and he saw the disciples up front talking with Jesus. The disciples seemed to be arguing with Jesus about something but Jesus was being cool.

The disciples got into a huddle and when they came out of it they gave Jesus 5 loaves of bread and what looked like some fish. What were they up to now, Obadiah thought?

Then he saw Jesus take the bread and lift it up to the sky and bless it. Then Jesus took the bread and fish and broke it into pieces and gave it to the disciples. The disciples took the food with a look on their face like, "What are we suppose to do with this?"

Obadiah reached into his traveling bag and pulled out 3 loaves of bread and some salted fish his wife had packed for him. Next to him was a Samaritan family who had some fruit. He offered them some of his bread and they shared their fruit.

Obadiah looked around. People were sharing their food with each other, hugging each other, laughing and enjoying the feeling of community.

Jesus was looking out over the crowd and the disciples were standing next to him looking and smiling too. The disciples couldn't believe their eyes.

After everybody got full (and sleepy) they gathered up the leftover food. Obadiah counted 12 baskets of bread and lots of leftover fish.

Jesus thanked everybody for coming out and said the benediction.

Everybody in the crowd hugged each other again and wished each other a safe journey home.

Obadiah had finally heard and seen Jesus for himself and the idea about trying to go into business with Jesus never even crossed his mind.

What *was* on Obadiah's mind was the miracle he had just witnessed: how one man had made a community out of a crowd of strangers.

Obadiah was now saddened. Bringing us together like this, Obadiah thought, was what was going to get this Jesus killed.

NIGGERLIPS

"Niggerlips! Niggerlips!
Mary got some niggerlips!
Niggerlips! Niggerlips!
Mary got some niggerlips!"

Kids can be so cruel. Mary wasn't quite sure what a *"nigger"* was but she did know that the taunts and the name-calling hurt all the same.

Mary had went to the same school with the same kids since she was in kindergarten. Now that she was eight and in the 3rd grade *things* had changed. Her classmates' had had new experiences and new exposures; they had been exposed to new ideas and their vocabularies had expanded. And with their new knowledge <u>some</u> of them had became mean.

Mary didn't remember who it was who had first called her that name, but ever since September it seemed that all of her classmates had started calling her *"Niggerlips."*

Sometimes, one of her classmates would whisper the name, just so that Mary could hear:

"Niggerlips! Niggerlips!
Mary got sime niggerlips!,

and sometimes a group of them would chant it loud, on the playground, so that everyone could hear:

"Niggerlips! Niggerlips!
Mary got some niggerlips!

Mary didn't tell her mother or father about it. Mary didn't tell her older brothers and sister about it. Mary didn't even tell her teacher, Mrs. Green, about the taunting and name-calling, because Mary was ashamed. Mary was ashamed and she didn't even know why. She was ashamed of being ashamed, but Mary didn't know how to explain her shame to anyone. So, Mary became quiet and only talked when she was spoken to. And Mary stopped smiling.

Sometimes Mary would look at herself in the mirror. She didn't look any different than any ot the other children in her class.

She wasn't the tallest and she wasn't the shortest. She wasn't the skinniest and she wasn't the fattest. Her hair was light brown and her cheeks were rosy. Her nose was thin and her lips were red. Her clothes were always clean and neat. Mary didn't understand.

One Thursday Mary was alone playing in her living room. The television was on as Mary had been watching cartoons but now it was just keeping her company.

All of a sudden Mary heard the announcer say, *"We interrupt your regularly scheduled programming for this special report. It has just been reported to us that the Rev. Dr. Martin Luther King has been shot and killed in Memphis, Tennessee. Reports are sketchy at this point but it appears he was killed at the Lorraine Motel. It appears that this was the work of a single gunman."*

Mary wasn't sure she knew who Dr. King was so she kept on playing.

All through the day there was nothing on television and nothing on the radio except special reports on Dr. King and his killing.

Just before dinner Mary and her mother and father, her older brothers and sister were watching the reports on the television when a reporter was interviewing a shopkeeper in Memphis. The shopkeeper had a rifle and he was saying, "*Yeah you let one of them niggers come up in here talking about burning and looting my store! I'll send a couple of them niggers to hell! That Martin Luther Coon got what he deserved! I hope one of those niggers would come up in here!....*"

Then Mary saw images of Negro men and women breaking windows and running in the streets with tvs and radios, coats and lamps, and food. But Mary looked at their black faces. Mary looked at their lips.

Mary excused herself from the dining room table and ran upstairs to the bathroom. She locked the door behind her and she looked into the mirror. And for the first time Mary saw yes, her lips were red but they were also full and large, just like the black people she had just seen on television.

Now Mary understood what her classmates had been saying about her: she had lips like a Negro and Negroes weren't nice. There weren't any Negroes at Mary's school and there weren't any Negroes that she knew but Mary had heard that Negroes weren't nice and she had just seen on tv that Negroes stole and broke windows and should be avoided.

Now Mary understood why she should be ashamed, and she was.

The next day when Mary went to school the whole school was talking about nothing except Dr. King being killed.

But Mary had a new mission. Mary began to look at her teacher's and the other student's lips.

And for the first time Mary saw that most of the them had very thin lips, and some of them didn't seem to have any lips at all!

She realized that her classmates were right about her lips and that there was nothing she could do about them.

Mary was getting a book out of her locker in the hallway when one of her classmates brushed against her. Under his breath, just so that Mary could hear he whispered,

"Niggerlips! Niggerlips!
Mary got some niggerlips!"

He smirked and walked into the classroom. Mary curled her lips inward and closed her locker. Mary walked quietly into her classroom but she didn't say a thing.

BISHOP ABDULLAH

Hi, my name is Martin, Martin R. Williams, and I am 9 years old. Only my teachers and other people who don't know me or my family call me Martin though. Momma and Daddy and everybody else call me "Bishop," really "Bishop Abdullah," but now mostly Bishop.

Momma said that when I was a baby there was this wrestler that useta' come on T.V. called "Bishop Abdullah." I guess he was a bad guy or something.

Anyway, when I was a baby my hair wasn't grown in like it is now and she said I had a whole lot right on the top of my head …and then clean spots around that. Then I had some more hair sticking off from the sides.

I done seen some pictures of what she talking about but that baby sho' don't look like me!

Anyway, that wrestler, "Bishop Abdullah," his hair looked just like mine. I think she said one of my cousins started calling

---

me "Bishop Abdullah" and everybody else just fell right in 'cause he was fat and I was fat too back then.

Everybody just call me "Bishop" now. Anyway, that wrestler don't wrestle no more but I kinda like Bishop 'cause nobody else I know got that name.

I asked Momma about my real name but she said she didn't want to talk about it and to go ask Daddy. It's funny because nobody I know in our family got that name.

The first time I remember asking Daddy about my name he was kinda tired and didn't want to be bothered. He said something like, "How did you get the name Martin? 'Cause that's your name, boy! Is your name Harry or Pete or Jaspar? Naw, yo' name is Martin. What else you gonna be named but yo' name!?" Daddy be buggin' sometimes.

I knew what to do though. You see my Daddy hate the Buffalo Bills. I just waited 'til one Sunday when the Bills had just lost a close game to the Dolphins and I knew he would be in a good mood!

—

When I asked him about my name again at first he just looked at me, ...and then pushed the recliner back so that the footrest came up.

Then Daddy said, "I named you Martin after one of the first black men I learned about once I went to college. You see, I didn't learn much in school about Black History growing up. So the only black men I had ever heard tell of were Frederick Douglass and Booker T. Washington, W.E.B. DuBois and George Washington Carver. But back in the 1800s there was this *baaaaad* black man named Martin Robison Delaney.

Him and Frederick Douglass was running buddies and they put out that newspaper, *The Northstar,* together. And talk about militant! Delaney was militant before militant was in style!

He was a doctor, went to Africa looking for land for black people to move to; he wrote four books, and was the highest ranking black officer in the US army during the Civil War."

"Hmph, yo' Momma wanted to name you Curtiss, after her brother. I named you Martin right then and there while she was holding you in the hospital room. You had a look about ya'." He paused and then said, "That was before you started gettin' older and losin' the little bit of sense you was born with!"

Daddy laughed a little and told me some other things about Martin Robison Delaney and what college was like....

Now I'm just waitin' 'til we start talkin' about the Civil War in school so that I can let everybody in my classroom know I was named after Martin Robison Delaney and tell them everything Daddy told me.

Oh yeah, and now I can't wait to go to college so that I can learn all about Black History too, just like my Daddy did!!

"SNEAZA"

During the 1950's and 1960's black people came up with alot of slogans. They came up with slogans like *"Black Power"*, and *"Black is Beautiful"*. Remember them? And who can forget, *"Say it loud, I'm black and I'm proud"*. James Brown came out with that song and messed up some of our worlds, didn't he?!

Now the reason black folks came up with those slogans in the Fifties and Sixties is because before then, in general, black folks didn't want to have nothing to do with being black!

Before the Fifties and Sixties most black folks had a real problem in identifying themselves with things black and African.

Most of the stories you hear about young black men growing up in the Sixties are about black boys growing up in the cities. I'm going to flip the script a little bit and tell you a story about a young black boy growing up in the Sixties out in rural Wayne County, out in Williamson, New York, out in *"The Core of Apple Country."*

This black boy's name was Sneaza. Now Sneaza was his nick-name. And if every black person would be honest they know they have a nick-name somewhere too!

Sneaza was in sixth grade. Sneaza's sixth-grade teacher was Mrs. Brownell.

One Monday morning Mrs. Brownell announced a special history assignment to the class. *"Your assignment will be to ask your parents or grandparents from what country your ancestors came from. You should also try to find out some interesting facts about that country. Your report will be due next Monday."*

The whole class was excited, except for Sneaza. Sneaza immediately felt sick. Sneaza realized that he had a really big problem. He was the only black child in his class. Sneaza knew that if he stood in that class next Monday morning and said his ancestor's came from Africa he would be the laughing stock of that class, he would be the laughing stock of the school, he would be the laughing stock of the whole county!

Sneaza had a real big problem.

—

But Sneaza got what most folks would call a "good education" out in Wayne County, out in Williamson, N.Y., out in *"The Core of Apple Country."* A good education meant that Sneaza could read, and write, and do arithmetic, but most of all it meant that Sneaza could think....and problem solve....

Sneaza got some history books from the library and he did some research on his own.

Time come and time go and Monday came around.

Mrs. Brownell stood in front of the class. "All right, class it's time for us to begin our special reports on your ancestors. Suzie, would you like to begin please?"

"Yes, thank you, Mrs. Brownell," Susan said. Susan was quite hyperactive and lively in her report. "I found out that my ancestors came from England, Mrs. Brownell. I found out that one of my relatives in England actually was royalty. That means that I'm royalty, too, Mrs. Brownell! I also found out that at one time the English people had a saying, *"the sun never set on the British Empire."* And that meant that the

British people owned land all over the world and there wasn't anywhere the sun shined that the British people weren't in control!"

"Thank you Suzie for that excellent report," Mrs. Brownell said.

Mrs. Brownell went around the class and the children reported their ancestors came from Ireland and Germany, Norway and Italy, and so on until finally it was Sneaza's turn.

"Sneaza, can you please stand and give us your report?" The whole class became suddenly quiet. Sneaza thought he heard a girl giggle behind him.

"Yes, Mrs. Brownell. I did some research from a history book I got from the school library. What I found out was that in 1619 a Dutch man-of-warre, really a battleship, came to Jamestown, Virginia."

"Off of that ship 20 colored people were sold to the people of Jamestown as indentured servants. This was the first documented time black people came to this country So since this was a Dutch ship and my ancestors were on it I assume my ancestors were *black Dutchmen!*"

The whole class was completely silent. Even Mrs. Brownell was at a loss for words. After a moment Mrs. Brownell said, "Thank you, Sneaza, for that <u>very</u> interesting report. Ah, Jimmy, are you ready to give your report?"

Sneaza, and many other black students of his generation, later learned that Africa had made many great and important contributions to the world.

Those students went to college and studied and discussed Ancient Egypt, and Imhotep, and Garvey and DuBois, and Noble Drew Ali.

Many of those students from the Sixties were finally able, after alot of reading and talking, to learn to appreciate all peoples' cultures and, most importantly, to accept that they had nothing to be ashamed of for being born black and a descendant of Africa.

WIND

Once Wind became a man. When Wind was a man he was a very rich man. Wind was a rich man from birth. Wind did not want from anything. But Wind was not happy. Wind would sigh.

One day one of Wind's friends came to visit. Wind asked his visitor, "What is wrong with me? Of all the things I possess known give me happiness!" And Wind would sigh.

Wind's friend thought for a moment and then said, "Like the floating bird, you yearn to be free. Do what they do, and you become free. Possess joy!"

Wind observed the birds he saw, and Wind realized that birds were partner with the Earth, needing one another....to survive... This could not be freedom, Wind thought, or make me happy.

Not long after this another of Wind's friends came to visit. Wind asked this friend, "What is wrong with me?

Of all the things I possess none give me happiness!" And Wind would sigh.

This friend thought a moment too, and then he replied, "Because you are a man you must meet death and become Wind again. Then, and only then, will you be happy."

Wind observed death: in the fields, in the cities, everywhere and always moving, and moving. And Wind found life and rebirth everywhere death had been.

And prepared and on purpose Wind left man and became Wind again.

Wind became the breeze that warms through and through; Wind became the cyclone that destroys; the hawk in the winter; Wind became the whispers in the middle of the night...and Wind is happy again, being Wind, and no longer sighs at all...!

OPPORTUNITY IS A
FOUR LETTER WORD

The older I get the more convinced I am that all the people on the face of this earth are one big family. Archaeologists and anthropologists can debate all they want!

Scientists can come up with all the theories they want about race and origins but I believe we are all the same, all one big family because of the fact of *STORY*!!

We are all *STORYTELLERS*, everywhere we are. We remember the past through *STORY*, we share the present through *STORY*, we have hope for the future through *STORY*.

STORY is one of the things that separate us from the animals. People produce *STORY*; animals are the product of *STORY*!!! Remember the wise owl, the wily rabbit, and clever fox??

This story is a slice of the *STORY* we call *WORLD HISTORY*! It is a sliver of *African American History* and a chunk of *Snead Family History*.

I call this story *"Opportunity is a Four Letter Word."* Sometimes opportunity means *MORE*. Sometimes opportunity means *LESS*!!

Joseph Alfred Snead, Sr. passed from this world to the next on April 11, 1944. He had not been doing well most of March and died in April of what was then called the *"Dropsy."* It was probably some kind of heart ailment.

He left to mourn his passing his wife, *Ruby Clark Snead*, and his *10 children*. *Ma*, as Ruby came to be known, was 8 months pregnant and gave birth to *Carter Snead* on May 10, 1944, 29 days after Joseph, Sr. had died. *Carter* was named after one of *Joseph Sr.'s* brothers.

The oldest sister, *Betty*, was already married and out of the house. The oldest son, *John "Bud" Snead*, was 18 years old when *Joseph Sr.* died.

Bud would help "get the farm in" in 1944, live in *Savannah, Georgia* the winter of 1944; help "get the farm in" in 1945 and then leave the household for good after that.

—

You see, **Ma** and her family were sharecroppers in **Sylvania, Georgia,** in **Scriven County.** When **Joseph Sr.** had died the family had already been loaned the money by the landlord for the year and they were in debt.

The Sneads raised *cotton* and *peanuts* to sell, but raised almost everything else they needed to live on their farm.

They had *chickens,* and *goats,* and *hogs,* and *cows.* The rest of the children living in the household were **Hattie Mae, Fannie Mag, Sadie, Joseph Jr., Linzzie Frank, Carroll, Walter, Melvin Lee,** and **Carter.**

Joseph Jr. was 13 years old when **Joseph Sr.** died. **Jimbo,** as he would become known, would only go to the **2nd grade** as he was needed more on the farm than in the classroom.

By **1949** Jimbo realized that he too had had enough of sharecropping and was looking for opportunity somewhere. This time *opportunity* meant *less:* less *backbreaking sharecropping,* less *long days,* less *dependence on him to be the man of the house, responsible for himself and his younger brothers and sisters.*

Joseph also realized the only way he was going to get Ma to leave the farm and sharecropping was if he left.

So in *1949 Joseph* moved to *Savannah, Georgia* and lived with Ma's first cousin, *Jean Mincy*, and her husband, *Harold*.

Joseph didn't have any work skills outside of farm work but he eventually became a body and fender man, working in an auto collision shop. So *Joseph* moved from the *rural South* to the *urban South* in search of *opportunity*, and found it.

Joseph also found love in *Savannah*. He met *Martha Tyler* in *1951* in Savannah. They were married and eventually had 3 sons: *Austin, Robert*, and *Vincent*.

Fannie Mag, one of *Joseph's older sisters*, had moved to New York State in *1948 or 1949*. She would eventually convince Ma to do the same.

By *1952 and 1953* Ma and the rest of the children still at home had moved to *New York State*.

—

In *May of 1956 Fannie Mag* and her husband, *Horace Daniels* came to *McCray, Georgia*, to attend the funeral of one of Horace's sister. They came through Savannah on their way North, going home.

Joseph and Martha talked with them. Without a lot of planning, and treating the trip more like a vacation than anything *Joseph and Martha* and their three sons piled into the car with *Horace and Fannie Mag* and headed North.

Joseph didn't have many friends who were heading North, out of the South. He didn't realize that he was a part of the *Great 1950s Migration of African Americans out of the South going to the West, Midwest, and North.*

But he and Martha were in search of *opportunity.* This time opportunity meant *MORE*: more *money* from working; more *educational opportunities* for their children; more *respect* from your employers.

Joseph thought they were going to be living in New York City!!

When he and his family arrived in *Ontario, New York on Memorial Day, 1956* (in rural *Wayne County)*, he was surprised!

But *Joseph* eventually began to like the country. It reminded him of growing up in rural Georgia, but without the sharecropping!

Both he and Martha got *jobs paying more than a $1.00 an hour and they were on their way!*

This chunk of *Snead family history* is the story of one family's move from the rural South, to the urban South, and then to the rural North.

This is a *story* that connects to all those other personal history *stories* which make the one big family we call *HUMANITY!!!!!*

RETOLD STORIES

THE WRESTLING MATCH

A long, long, long, long, long, long, long time ago, in the kingdom of Mali, in the city of Djeriba, in northeast Africa, lived Yakubu.

Yakubu was a very rich man. But not only was Yakubu a rich man, Yakubu was also a greedy man. And not only was Yakubu a rich man *and* a greedy man, Yakubu was also a fool!

Let us remember Yakubu's story so that we may discern right from wrong.

Yakubu lived in a large, beautifully built stone palace, with many rooms and servants. The wall protecting his palace was as thick as the wall protecting the city itself.

Colorful brocade drapes hung in his rooms. Imported carpets covered his floors. Soft goatskin cushions and silk pillows were placed on the carpets for his courtiers and guests. Yakubu sat on a finely crafted, gold-inlaid stool with lions carved in each leg.

Yakubu wore the finest silk and woven cotton tunics and pants money could buy.

Yakubu had the freshest food: fish, meats, melons, dates, olives, and grains. Any food his heart desired he could have.

And Yakubu had several wives, one more beautiful than the other. And he had many strong and healthy children.

But Yakubu treated his servants with contempt and he treated his wives and children like servants.

The courtiers, always trying to please Yakubu and stay in his favor, always agreed with him, no matter what he proclaimed.

They behaved this way because Yakubu was a rich man, and he was a greedy man, and because he was a fool.

Once a month or so Yakubu would give a banquet for his courtiers. Because Yakubu was lavish in his feasting the courtiers would come and partake of the food and dolo, a strong drink that warmed the body and dimmed the mind.

After Yakubu had guzzled several cups of dolo down he would boldly declare to all those in attendance: "Gold is the best friend a man can have! Give me gold dust from the Sudan and I can do the rest!"

The revellers would salute Yakubu and applaud his utterances. The festivities lasted late into the night.

Now one of Yakubu's new servants was a young man from outside the walls of the city, and a day's journey. His name was Bilal. Bilal worked diligently at learning his responsibilities in the palace.

When Bilal was paid his salary he would take almost all of his earnings home to his mother and father, his sisters and his brothers, who still lived outside the walls of the city.

Bilal was a quick learner and succeeded in mastering his tasks in very little time.

Yakubu took to watching Bilal working and thought to himself, "This one is not lazy like the rest of my servants. I have yet to see him steal anything from me. I would love to have Bilal be my servant, forever, for free!

I must think of a way to accomplish this." So Yakubu set his mind to designing a plan to transform Bilal into his slave.

One day, when returning from a visit to his home, Bilal was walking in the woods near

---

Yakubu's palace. It was then that Bilal saw a clump of wood. Bilal went over and inspected the piece of wood closely. The more he studied it the more the piece of wood resembled a small statue of a man.

It was the custom in those days that everyone should have an Ancestor statue in their home or room.

Having an Ancestor statue always in view helped remind the living of the sacrifices, struggles, and contributions made by the ancestors for the people existing today.

But Bilal was so poor that he did not even own an Ancestor statue.

He took the clump of wood back to his room, bathed it, and rubbed shea butter and perfume into it. Then he arranged an altar for his Ancestor statue on the East wall of his room.

Everyday Bilal poured libation at the foot of his altar. Everyday Bilal brought fresh water and food to his Ancestor statue. Everyday Bilal prayed and meditated and remembered the worthiness and fidelity of the ancestors.

Early one morning, not long after Bilal

had set up his altar, three of Yakubu's other servants entered Bilal's room.

When these three servants saw Bilal meditating in front of the clump of wood they began to make fun of him saying, "Bilal has found a *free* Ancestor statue in the woods!"

"Surely the ancestors will bless him for his *great* investment!" one of the servants said sarcastically.

The loud voices and laughter of the three servants caused such a commotion that Yakubu himself came to see what was going on.

When Yakubu saw Bilal's altar and wooden Ancestor statue a plan to make Bilal his servant, forever, for free leapt into his mind!

When Yakubu had entered Bilal's room all of the servants had become mute and lowered their eyes towards the dirt floor.

"Bilal. *Bilal*! I would like to make you an offer," Yakubu purred haughtily, pacing proudly back and forth, barely looking in Bilal's direction. "I would like to suggest a wrestling match. I would like to suggest that *your* Ancestor statue wrestle *my* Ancestor statue."

Yakubu almost burst into a jeering laughter himself while speaking!

"If *your* Ancestor statue defeats *my* Ancestor statue in the wrestling match, I will give you my palace and all of the things within it," Yakubu smirked.

"No, I will give you more! I will give you my palace, my clothing, and all of the food I possess," Yakubu offered.

"No! I will not only wager my palace, my clothing, and all of my food. I will also give to you my gold, my servants, my wives and my children if your Ancestor statue defeats my Ancestor statue in the wrestling match," Yakubu concluded, majestically raising both arms above his head.

"But, Bilal, if my Ancestor statue defeats your Ancestor statue in the wrestling match you must be my servant, forever, for free!" And having thus spoken Yakubu clasped his hands behind his back, stood still, and stared in the direction of the door, waiting for Bilal's response.

Bilal was silent. But Bilal's placid face belied the tumult in his heart.

Bilal had heard that Yakubu had a solid gold Ancestor statue with diamond eyes. He had heard that Yakubu kept it hidden secretly away for fear of it being stolen.

Yakubu, it was said, displayed the solid gold Ancestor statue with the diamond eyes once a year, and then only on the most Holy of days. Even then Yakubu never let the statue out of his sight.

Bilal thought, "If I accept this offer and my Ancestor statue loses the wrestling match I will have to become Yakubu's servant, forever, for free. If I refuse his offer he is surely to become angry with me and dismiss me from his palace. Then who will support my father and mother, my sisters and my brothers?" Bilal was silent.

Yakubu began pacing again, agitated that Bilal had not responded to his proposal.

"Bilal! *Bilal!*" Yakubu sneered, "I have made you an offer and I swear on my father's name before these servants and the ancestors that all of these things will be yours if your Ancestor statue defeats my ancestor statue."

"What is your response, Bilal!?" Yakubu demanded.

Bilal was silent. "Very well then, Bilal!" Yakubu seethed, "I will take your silence for acceptance of my offer! Meet me in the courtyard to commence the match!"

Yakubu strode out of Bilal's room as if staying a moment longer might contaminate him with some unknown disease.

The three servants looked one to the other and then at Bilal. They were regretful that they had caused this predicament for Bilal.

As each silently left Bilal's room they touched him slightly on his left shoulder with their left hand as a sign of their misery.

Now left alone, Bilal decided to finish his morning meditations. Bilal had just shut his eyes when he heard a voice that he had never heard before. The voice said, "Don't worry

Bilal, we will win!" Bilal opened his eyes and there, to his amazement, was his Ancestor statue smiling down at him. Bilal closed his eyes and thanked the ancestors for this sign.

Bilal finished his meditations, picked up his wooden Ancestor statue, and went into the courtyard. All of Yakubu's courtiers were in the courtyard. His servants stood a respectful distance behind them.

Yakubu had already ordered the wrestling circle drawn in the dirt. In the center of the circle was Yakubu's solid gold Ancestor statue with the diamond eyes. Bilal placed his wooden Ancestor statue inside the wrestling circle and stood back. Magically the Ancestor statues came alive!

The solid gold Ancestor statue with the diamond eyes stretched its huge, bulging, gold muscles. Its diamond eyes glinted in the sunlight. Then the solid gold Ancestor statue assumed the wrestler's crouch and began to push the wooden Ancestor statue, trying to maneuver it outside of the circle. The wooden Ancestor statue kept its balance and simply allowed itself to be pushed around and backwards within the circle.

The courtiers and Yakubu were clamoring for the solid gold Ancestor statue to make quick work of the wooden Ancestor statue.

"Win! Win! You *must* win!" shouted Yakubu over the whoops of his courtiers.

When the wrestling match had begun the sun was high up in the sky, now it was setting in the west.

The solid gold Ancestor statue was still pushing and shoving the wooden Ancestor statue, but not with the energy it once had had. The solid gold Ancestor statue was covered with sweat and it took in great gulps of air.

Now the wooden Ancestor statue began to pull on the solid gold Ancestor statue, grabbing its elbows. Pulling and tugging on the solid gold Ancestor statue the wooden Ancestor statue backed around the circle faster and faster, and faster until it locked its right arm underneath the left shoulder of the solid gold Ancestor statue, and twisted sharply to its left.

"Huh-jahhh!" the wooden ancestor statue yelled. The solid gold Ancestor statue's feet left the ground, its body becoming airborne. Out of the wrestling circle it landed, rolling over several times, in a cloud of dust.

"*Nooo!!! No!!!!!*" Yakubu screamed, "*Noooo!!!!!*" But it was too late, the match was over. The courtiers, the servants, Yakubu's wives and children, (who had come to see the outcome of the wrestling match), were all silent.

Yakubu went into the palace and gazed at all of the possessions that once were his but now belonged to Bilal.

Yakubu came out of the palace, gathered up his solid gold Ancestor statue with the diamond eyes, and without a word, began to trudge slowly towards the gates of the palace.

Not looking back, Yakubu left the grounds of the palace and its walls. As Yakubu made his way from the palace he heard behind him a cry go up: "Long live Bilal! Long live Bilal! Long live Bilal!"

And Yakubu thought that he heard the voices of his courtiers, his wives and children mixed with those of his servants in the chanting.

Yakubu quickly realized that he had made no friends in Djeriba as door after door was closed in his face.

Yakubu applied to learn the trade of a weaver to support himself. When the owner saw Yakubu's fine clothing, fat stomach, and soft hands the owner said, "No, no, no. This one has never done hard work. This one will not do."

Yakubu undertook to become a wood carver, and then a barber, and still later a farmer. But each time the proprietor would say, "No, no, no. This one has never done hard work. This one will not do."

After many weeks and months Yakubu was reduced to fighting with dogs for scraps of food and muddy water in the streets.

One day long after the wrestling match Yakubu was sitting near a stream of water. He saw his reflection in the water,....and began to cry. His clothes were ragged and dirty. His body was unwashed and thin. His face was unshaven, and his hair unoiled and scraggly.

Yakubu reached into his pouch and brought out his solid gold Ancestor statue with the diamond eyes. He placed it on the ground in front of him.

"It is your fault I have been brought to this state!" accused Yakubu. "If you had not lost the wrestling match I would still have my palace, my clothes and food, my gold and servants and wives. It is *your* fault!"

The solid gold Ancestor statue with the diamond eyes replied, "Do not blame me, my friend. Do not blame me! I was kept locked away all year long, except for one day out of the year. "

"Every day Bilal poured libation to his ancestors. Every day Bilal brought fresh water and food to his Ancestor statue. Every day Bilal prayed and meditated and remembered the sacrifices, struggles, and contributions of his ancestors. That gave his wooden Ancestor statue strength."

"Even though his Ancestor statue was made of wood the ancestors were well pleased with Bilal and bestowed his wooden Ancestor statue with endurance."

"How often did you feed me? How often did <u>you</u> pour libation to the ancestors? How often did you pray and meditate and remember the worthiness of your ancestors?"

"Although made of gold, my strength was ephemeral. Your faith in the ancestors was small and weak, and that rendered me feeble and faint. Do not blame me, my friend."

Yakubu lowered his head in shame. He realized that the solid gold Ancestor statue with the diamond eyes was right.

Once he had been blessed with material wealth and a life of ease. Now he was blessed to perceive what a fool he had been.

Yakubu understood finally that when you respect, remember, and recall the virtues of the ancestors, the ancestors supply patience and peacefulness, power and purity to you.

THE MAN AND THE WOMAN

In the beginning God created Man and Woman equal in all ways. God gave Man and Woman a beautiful yellow, split-level ranch house and told them to be fruitful and multiply. And multiply they did. In no time at all their beautiful house was full of children.

Since Man and Woman had been created equal in all ways they did the same kind of jobs. There wasn't no Man's work or Woman's work, they each did whatever needed to be done.

The biggest problem was though that since Man and Woman had equal strength they would get to fussing sometimes and because Man could not "Hold Woman Down" and Woman could not "Hold Man Down" neither one was satisfied! And it went on like this for a long time.

One hot, balmy summer day Man was outside just finishing up a nice load of white wash and he had just hung up the last of the sheets on the line and he had a taste for a nice long, cool, cold glass of water.

He went into the house and opened up the refrigerator door and there was the water jug....bone dry.

"Doggone that Woman! She always drinking the last of the water and then putting the empty water jug back in the refrigerator! I'm so tired of her! I'm going up to Heaven and have a talk with God about this!"

Well, when Man got to the Pearly Gates he knocked nicely and God said, "Come on in, Man, what's on your mind?"

"Heavenly Father, creator of all that we see, and the author of all we know. Father, it was you who put that blazing ball we call the Sun in it's place and told it to stay! Because of you, Father, Time comes and Time go and Man has to get with it or get out of the way. Father, I'm coming to you as a bad child before a good parent asking that you find it in your heart to answer this prayer."

God kind of liked the way Man was praying so He said, "Well what is it Man? What is it that you want?"

"Father, I need MORE STRENGTH so I can make that Woman you gave me mind. That way Father you would not have to be coming down seeing about us all the time when we get into those little spats ....and that would take a load off your schedule, Lord!!"

God was in a generous mood that day and said, "OK Man, you got it! You now have MORE STRENGTH than woman!"

Man told God thank you kindly and took off for earth. He couldn't wait to show Woman who was boss now!

Time Man hit the front door he started talking trash.

"Woman, come on over here and meet your Master! From now on when I say jump all I want you to do is ask me how high!!" Woman looked at Man out of the corner of her eye, put her hand over her mouth and yawned.

Man grabbed Woman's wrist and slowly she realized that she could not break his grip. A look of amazement came over her face and Man was all smiles.

"How did you do that?" Woman asked surprised as Man released her wrist. Woman dusted herself off, spit in both palms of her hands and rubbed them together, and did some quick stretches.

"Come on Man, you got lucky on that one!!" Woman reached out, Man grabbed hold of her wrist again and Woman was again unable to break his grip. Man released Woman and she cussed. Upset and angry she asked, "How are you able to hold me down?!"

"I asked God for MORE STRENGTH and He gave it to me." Man had a big smile on his face. "And he put me in charge! So from now on you just do what I say and I don't want to hear no back talk!"

Well Woman was very upset by now and she went straight up to Heaven. Woman didn't even knock on the Pearly Gates, she just walked straight into God's living room!

Woman asked God, "God, why did you give Man MORE STRENGTH?! Now he down there making me do things I don't want to do!

—

Please God give me MORE STRENGTH too so we can be equal again!"

God knew Woman was upset so He overlooked her bad manners.

"Woman, what I give I don't take away. I gave Man MORE STRENGTH and no matter how strong you get Man will always have MORE STRENGTH than you from now on!"

Well Woman didn't like this answer too much so she just turned her back on God, walked out, and slammed the Pearly gates behind her!

Just as Woman got outside the Pearly Gates who should she run into but the Devil. The Devil looked Woman up and down and he could tell that his services were needed.

"What's up sugar?" the Devil purred. "Why you looking all mean and upset, girl?"

The Woman told him all about how God had given Man MORE STRENGTH and how now he was holding her down.

69

The Devil said, "Girl it ain't no big thing! Since God done gave Man something He got to give you something too! I want you to go back to God and ask Him for the keys that are hanging over His fireplace. You get the keys and I'll show you what to do with them!"

So Woman went back to the Pearly Gates and knocked real polite this time. God said, "Come on in Woman. What can I do for you now?"

Woman was as sweet and sugary as a bowl of honey. "Father God, you was there before there was Day. You are the Light of the World. On you we all depend and can't do a thing without your grace. You can make the rough places smooth and the crooked places straight. I need you to answer my prayer this morning Father!"

"What's on your mind Woman?"

"Since you gave Man something I was wondering could you give me those old keys hanging by the fireplace?"

Woman's prayer had touched God's heart. "Sure Woman. Here they are." God gave Woman the keys and she thanked Him and left.

The Devil was waiting on her and time she got outside the Pearly Gates they started to walk back to Earth. The Devil started teaching Woman what to do with the keys.

"Now see this green key?' he said, "this green key is the key to the kitchen. You know that Man of yours loves to eat! When you get back to your house I want you to lock the door to the kitchen. Lock it up tight!"

The Devil continued, "This red key is the key to the bedroom. And you know how Man loves his sleep ....and his pleasures, right? Take this red key and lock that door too!"

Woman asked, "Lock it up?" The Devil grinned and nodded.

The Devil continued, "See this black key? This is the key to Man's children and you know he don't want to be cut off from them! Lock all of his children away from him too."

"Lock up my babies?" Woman asked. "Lock 'em up!" the Devil replied.

"Now this is the most important part," the Devil concluded. "After you get through locking up those doors I want you to go have a seat and do not say a thing to Man until he comes to you!! You understand?" Woman grinned and said yes.

Well, Woman locked up all those doors just like the Devil told her to.

When Man did get home Woman was sitting under a shade tree with her eyes closed, singing a song Man had never heard before:

"The blues is about a man,
don't know right from wrong.
The blues is about a man,
who don't know right from wrong.
I've got the keys in my pocket.
Waitin' for my Man to get home!"

Well Man just went right on into the house and the first thing he noticed was that the kitchen door was locked. He tried the door knob but it wouldn't budge. Man took his shoulder and tried to knock the door open but he couldn't do it, it was too strong.

Then Man went upstairs to their bedroom and he noticed that the bedroom door was locked too! Man tried twisting the door knob and busting the door down but was unable to do that either!

Right after that he realized that he didn't see his children running around the house or yard. Man went to the children's bedroom and he could hear them talking and playing on the other side of the door. Man turned the door knob and it was locked! Man tried to knock the door open with his shoulder but it wouldn't give!

Man ran back out to the shade tree where Woman was sitting still singing with her eyes closed. "Woman! Woman, who locked up all those doors in the house?!!"

Woman yawned softly and nonchalantly replied, "Oh, I did. I used these here keys." Woman dangled the keys in Man's face.

"But where did you get those keys from?"

"God gave them to me,....but the Devil showed me how to use them!!"

Man was pacing up and down and becoming more and more upset. "All right now Woman, come on and open up those doors before you make me do something I don't want to do!!" he said, huffing and puffing.

Woman crossed her arms and refused to unlock the doors until Man promised not to hold her down anymore.

Man and Woman started fussing with one another something fierce. Man threatened to hold Woman down forever and Woman threatened to never cook again, never let Man get another good night of rest, and to never let him near his children again.

The fussing was getting to the point that all of Creation was in an uproar. The grass stopped growing, petals started falling off of flowers and the birds refused to sing.

Then the booming voice of God spoke from the cloud:

"Man!! Woman!! Y'all stop that fussing right now! Y'all hear me?!!"

Man and Woman stood still with their heads bowed in the presence of God. "Yes Lord," they responded in unison.

God said to Man "Man, when I gave you MORE STRENGTH I didn't give it to you so that you could hold Woman down. I gave you MORE STRENGTH so that you could lift Woman up!

From now on I want you to use that MORE STRENGTH to protect Woman and your family. You are to do the providing for your family and make sure that they are safe! Do you understand me?"

"Yes Lord," Man responded softly.

Then God said to Woman, "Woman, I didn't give you those keys so that you could lock up those doors. I gave you those keys so that you could keep those doors forever open!"

"From now on it is your job to make sure that your home is one of joy and happiness. It is your job to nurture your Man and children and keep your family together. Do you understand me?"

"Yes Lord, " Woman said.

"This day I am creating two new things: Respect and Compromise."

"Man and Woman whenever you two live together from now on Respect and Compromise shall live with you ....otherwise ain't gonna be nothing but trouble!"

"No matter what y'all always respect one another and yourselves! And when you have a disagreement both of you gotta be willing to listen to the other one and compromise. Y'all understand?" Both Man and Woman nooded their heads. "That will make any house GOOD!" God said smiling.

Both Man and Woman did understand and from that day to this day when you find a Man and Woman living together and ain't no fussing and fighting going on you are sure to find Respect and Compromise living in that house with them.

THE BIG WIND

A long time ago animals did everything that you see people doing today on the face of the earth. In fact most animals were farmers.

Every day the animals would go out and plow their fields. Every day the animals would take all kinds of seeds and plants- corn, potatoes, watermelon seeds, cucumber seeds and more- and plant them. The sun would go up into the sky and the rain would come down and all of those plants would grow.

But one day the animals went out and they plowed their fields and planted their seeds but the sun was like a big ball of fire in the sky. The rain refused to come down for a long, long time. There was a drought in their land.

Because there was no food all of the animals got thinner, and thinner and thinner. And because there was no water the animals got thirstier, and thirstier and thirstier..

There was one place where there was water and there was food. At the end of a long road there was a pear tree with pears on it the

---

size of watermelons. The reason that those pears grew so big was because on the other side of the pear tree there was a pond that had not dried up.

But, there was a problem. There was a real big problem! At the foot of that pear tree there lived a mean, nasty, didn't-care-about-nobody-but-himself, wouldn't share with nobody no matter who asked him Bengal tiger.

Every time one of those animals would approach the pear tree or ask if they could have some of the pond water the Bengal tiger would roar, "Noooo!! Stay away from my pond water! Stay away from my pears!"

This went on for a long time and because those animals didn't have any food they got thinner, and thinner and thinner! Because they didn't have any water those animals got thirstier, and thirstier and thirstier!

One day a stranger visited the land where the drought was. The animals could tell he was a stranger because of the way he walked, he had his hat on backwards, and his pants were sagging a bit so that you could see the top of his underwear. This stranger's name was "Bruh Rabbit."

Well Bruh Rabbit saw how thin and thirsty all of the animals were and they began to tell him about the drought and about the Bengal tiger who would not allow any of them to have any of his pears or water from his pond.

Bruh Rabbit was smart and tricky. Just like that he came up with a plan to help those animals get some of those pears and some of that pond water. Bruh Rabbit went around to each one of those animals and whispered his plan in each one of their ears. Then he told each one of them to, "Meet me in the morning when the dew is still on the ground!"

The next morning when the dew was still wet on the ground all of those animals gathered in a field with Bruh Rabbit. Bruh Rabbit divided the animals into three groups: the animals with nice deep voices he told to say as loud as they could, *"Boom! Boom!"* Those animals with strong arms he told to pick up a stick and strike a log or tree, *"Bam! Bam!"*

Those animals with feathers (birds) he told to go up in the trees and make a flapping sound with their wings, *"Wooosh! Wooosh!"*

Bruh Rabbit told the animals that when he counted to three he wanted each of them to *"Boom! Boom! Bam! Bam! and Wooosh! Wooosh!"* as loud as they could until he told them to stop.

Bruh Rabbit counted to three and all of those animals began to "Boom! Boom!, Bam! Bam! and Wooosh! Wooosh as loud as they could. It sounded like the end of the world! Finally Bruh Rabbit said stop and all of the animals did.

Then Bruh Rabbit told the animals, "I am going to go up this road to meet that Bengal tiger. When you hear me say, *"I have to go"* I want you to make that same noise again for at least 2 minutes." All of the animals agreed.

Bruh Rabbit grabbed a rope and put it over his left shoulder and started walking down the road to the pear tree and pond where the Bengal tiger lived.

When the Bengal tiger saw Bruh Rabbit approaching he ran to him and said, "Hello stranger. I was sleeping when I was woken up by this terrible noise that sounded like thunder! Then I saw the trees moving and shaking like a hurricane... Do you know what is going on?"

Bruh Rabbit replied, "Oh, you can call me Bruh Rabbit. Yessir, there is a "big wind" coming and it is going to blow everything off of the face of the earth. I have this rope here and I am on my way to go tie one of my friends down.

Well the Bengal tiger was mean and nasty but he wasn't stupid. He thought: a big wind comes and blows everything off of the face of the earth...it will blow me away too! The Bengal tiger started to plead with Bruh Rabbit to tie him down.

Bruh Rabbit responded, "I'm sorry sir. I can't tie you down with this rope. This rope is for my friend. In fact, I don't have time to talk *"I have to go!"*

When those animals heard that they began to *"Boom! Boom! Bam! Bam! Wooosh! Wooosh!"* again as loud as they could. When the animals finally stopped the Bengal tiger was almost in tears.

"Please Bruh Rabbit," the Bengal tiger begged, "I don't want to get blown off of the face of the earth! Please tie me down! Please!" Bruh Rabbit responded, "No, no, no. This rope is for my friend who lives up the road."

The Bengal tiger continued to plead with Bruh Rabbit until finally Bruh Rabbit agreed to tie the Bengal tiger down so that he would not get blown off of the face of the earth.

The Bengal tiger stood next to a tall tree and Bruh Rabbit wrapped the rope around him and the tree.

Bruh Rabbit tied the rope around his ankles, he tied it around his knees, he tied the rope around the Bengal tiger's waist, and he tied it around the Bengal tiger's neck. Bruh Rabbit pulled the rope tightly around the Bengal tiger and asked him was the rope tight enough?

"Well, it is a little too tight around my neck," the Bengal tiger replied. I can't hardly move a muscle."

"That's good!" Bruh Rabbit responded. "Look at you. You are all tied up because you wouldn't share any of your pond water or any of your pears with your community!"

Bruh Rabbit told all of the other animals to come out of hiding. The animals began to eat those juicy pears and some of them even did the back-float in the pond. All of the animals got their fill of pears and water.

Eventually the rain came down again and the drought ended. Eventually all of those animals went back to being farmers. Eventually that rope fell off of that mean and nasty Bengal tiger and he was so ashamed that he hadn't shared his pears and pond water with the other animals that he scurried away and no one ever saw him again.

But that day all of those animals learned a great lesson. Those animals learned that no matter how big, how mean, or how nasty a problem was that when they all worked together that they could overcome any problem that they were faced with.

Those animals learned that when they all worked together there was no problem that they couldn't solve!

SNAKE AND HUNTER

Not so long ago there was a huge and destructive fire in the forest. The fire caused so much damage in the forest that all of the animals had to scurry about, trying to find a place to hide.

Even old mean, nasty, poisonous Bruh Snake had to try to find a place to hide. Just before the flames engulfed him he slithered down into a hole.

Well, the South Wind (Afer) blew dark, black rainclouds directly over the forest fire. When the clouds burst it was like buckets, it was like sheets of rain coming down on the fire and it put the fire out.

All of the animals came out of their hiding places to see how much damage had been done. It was at that point that Bruh Snake realized that he had a big problem..

The hole that he had slithered down into to get away from the fire was deep and the walls were steep and slippery. Try as he could he could not get himself up out of that hole.

So in his very, very nicest snake voice Bruh Snake began to call for help: "Help please. Help please! *Help please!!!*"

But none of the other animals would help Bruh Snake. Every one of them knew that Bruh Snake was so mean, he was so spiteful, he was so hateful that if they tried to help him get up out of that hole some way or another they would end up getting bit! They knew it! Every one of those animals walked by the hole that Bruh Snake was in just like they didn't hear him.

Finally a Hunter, walking in the forest, heard Bruh Snake's call for help. The Hunter went over to the hole Bruh Snake was in and reached his right arm down into the hole. Bruh Snake quickly wrapped himself around the Hunter's arm, the Hunter stood up and stepped back and was getting ready to let Bruh Snake go when Bruh Snake reared up and was getting ready to bite the Hunter!

The Hunter said, "Whoa, whoa, whoa!! I just got you up out of that hole. Why are you getting ready to bite me?" Bruh Snake responded, "Because, that's what snakes do!"

—

The Hunter said, "No, no, no! It is not right that you should return kindness with cruelty."

Bruh Snake thought for a moment and then he said, "Yes, but how can I be sure?"

Well the Hunter had never been asked a question like this and he thought about it for a moment and then he replied, "I know. Let us go ask King Anansi. King Anansi is a good judge and he is the wisest king in the land. He can tell us right from wrong. He shall know the answer..."

Bruh Snake sighed and agreed to let King Anansi decide right from wrong. Still wrapped around the Hunter's right arm Bruh Snake and the Hunter set off to the city where King Anansi lived.

The Hunter and Bruh Snake traveled all that day and arrived at the wall of King Anansi's city that evening. At the wall of the city the Hunter and Bruh Snake met a group of animals that were also waiting to enter King Anansi's city. In the group of animals there was a donkey, a cow and a horse.

Since both the animals and the Hunter and Bruh Snake had to wait before they would be allowed into the city the Hunter explained to the animals that Bruh Snake had been in a hole, that he had helped Bruh Snake out of the hole, and in return Bruh Snake now wanted to bite him! The Hunter asked each animal was it right to return kindness with cruelty?

Sister Cow said, "All of my life I have given Man my milk. From that milk Man has made cheese and butter. My owner and his family have been strong and healthy because of my milk. But just yesterday I heard my owner tell his friend that they were going to kill me, and chop my body up for steak and meat!"

When Bruh Snake heard this he reared up and said, "Seeeee!"

Brother Donkey spoke next. Brother Donkey said, "All of my life I've carried heavy loads on my back for my owner. All I have received in return for my service is to be called stupid and dumb, and beat with a stick. My owner told his friend when I die they are going to throw my body down an old abandoned well...!"

When Bruh Snake heard this he reared up again and said, "Seeeeeeee!!"

Brother Horse spoke next. He said, "Just like my cousin Bruh Donkey I too have carried heavy loads on my back for my owner. I have also plowed the fields for my owner and he and his family have gotten strong from the food they have raised. I know that when I die they will make wigs out my tail hair and glue from my hooves and soap from my body!"

When Bruh Snake heard this he could hardly contain himself. He reared up and said, "Seeeeeeeee!!!" and was getting ready to bite the Hunter when the Hunter said "No, you agreed we would ask King Anansi."

Finally the Hunter and Bruh Snake were allowed inside the city and King Anansi agreed to hear them in his palace.

Bruh Snake and the Hunter told their story to King Anansi about the forest fire and Bruh Snake becoming trapped in the hole. The Hunter told how he had helped Bruh Snake out of the hole and in return Bruh Snake wanted to bite him.

King Anansi sat and he listened and he thought. Finally he said, "I am not understanding what has happened. We must return to the site of these things you are telling me about so that you can show me what has happened, and I can see with my own eyes."

King Anansi gave the Hunter and Bruh Snake a comfortable bed for the evening and early the next day King Anansi, the Hunter and Bruh Snake traveled back to the forest where the fire had been. King Anansi said, "Show me what has happened."

They found the hole that Bruh Snake had crawled into to get away from the fire. The Hunbter kneeled down and allowed Bruh Snake to slither back into the hole and the Hunter stepped back.

Now because Bruh Snake knew that the Hunter and King Anansi were there he called out for help very calmly: "Help please.. Somebody please help me out of this hole. Come on Mr. Hunter help me out of this hole...."

The Hunter came back to the hole and was getting ready to put his arm back into the hole to help Bruh Snake out of the hole when King Anansi stopped the Hunter.

King Anansi said, "No Hunter, stop! I will now make my decision. Hunter, you are not to help Bruh Snake out of the hole this time. Bruh Snake must learn to appreciate a kind deed."

Bruh Snake began pleading and begging the Hunter to help him out of the hole. Then he realized that they had left.

Bruh Snake sat in the hole and then he stretched and tried to get out...but he was unable to. Bruh Snake sat in that hole for hours and stretched and tried to get out of the hole but he was unable to.

Then, just before Midnight, Bruh Snake stretched with all of his might and determination and he was just able to get his head over the lip of the hole and pull himself up out of the hole.

Snake had learned a valuable lesson.

A couple of days later Bruh Snake heard that the Hunter had gotten caught poaching on a nearby King's land and, to make an example of the Hunter, the King had decided to kill the Hunter.

Bruh Snake said to himself, "I must go and help my friend."

Snake slithered into the King's palace unseen and he went right up underneath the King's throne and he reached up and bit the King, right on his butt!

The King jumped up and in all of the ensuing confusion Bruh Snake slithered away and found the prison where the Hunter was being held.

Bruh Snake said to the Hunter, "A few days ago you did me a kindness. Since then I have learned to appreciate a kind act, and now I will show kindness to you." Bruh Snake smiled. "I have just bit the King, and he shall surely die within 24 hours."

Bruh Snake gave the Hunter a small calabash. "In this calabash," Bruh Snake con-

---

tinued, "is the only known cure for my bite.

Send word to the King that you have an antidote for my bite but that the only way that you will give it to him is if he frees you and gives you his only daughter's hand in marriage."

The Hunter sent word to the King, and mostly because the King didn't want to die, he agreed to the Hunter's offer.

The King took the antidote and was feeling fine within hours. Because this King was a King and a man of his word he freed the Hunter and gave him his only daughter's hand in marriage.

I can tell you that this whole story is true from the beginning to the end because I got drunk at the wedding!

AYO AND THE PALM WINE

Once upon a time in a small village in the nation of Ghana, west Africa, there lived a King. The King and the villagers loved one another. The King loved all of the people in his village and all of the people in his village loved the King.

One day the King called a big meeting with all of the people in the village. Once everyone was gathered the King looked out over all of the residents of his village and he said to them. "I love each and every one of you! I love each and every one of you so much that I have decided to give the whole village a party."

The King continued, "I will provide all of the meats and vegetables for the party. I will provide all of the desserts. All I want the men in my village to provide is a gourd full of palm wine."

Once the villagers had heard the King make this announcement they couldn't wait for the party. The King made his announcement Monday morning and the party was going to be Saturday evening.

Time come and time go. Saturday come around.

In this village lived a man named Ayo. When Ayo woke up late Saturday morning he looked high and he looked low but he could not find a drop of palm wine in his house. Ayo and some of his neighbors had been drinking palm wine late into Friday night and now all of his palm wine was gone. Ayo also did not have any money to buy any palm wine.

Ayo asked his wife what should he do. He did not want to be embarrassed when the party began that evening and be the only man who failed to bring palm wine.

Ayo's wife said, "Why don't you ask your neighbor to loan you some palm wine. Surely he will be willing to do that!" Ayo responded that that was a great idea and he went next door and knocked on his neighbor's door.

When Ayo's neighbor answered the knock Ayo said, "Neighbor! Greetings to you! You know the King's party is this evening and I have looked high and I have looked low but I cannot find a drop of palm wine in my house. Please Neighbor can you give me some palm wine to take to the party so that I will not be embarrassed?"

Ayo's neighbor looked away. You see, this was not the first time that Ayo had come asking to "borrow" palm wine from him. And to make matters worse Ayo was very slow in replacing the palm wine he had borrowed.

Ayo's neighbor replied, "Ayo, yes I do have palm wine for the party tonight. I tell you what: I will sell you some palm wine but I have none to give you...".

Ayo was furious! "What, you will <u>sell</u> me some palm wine to <u>give</u> away at a free party?! I do not think so!" Ayo turned and left his neighbor's house without another word!

Ayo told his wife what had happened at his neighbor's house. Ayo had his wife sat and they thought, and they thought and they sat. Time was drawing near for the party to begin and Ayo still did not have any palm wine for the party.

Ayo finally said to his wife, "I know what I will do. I will go down to the stream and fill my calabash with streamwater. When I pour my calabash of water into the large wine pot no one will know that it was not palm wine!" Ayo's wife agreed and that is exactly what Ayo did.

Time come and all of the men, women and children gathered in the center of the village for the King's party. The King was seated on his royal stool. Next to him were the royal drummers and musicians and singers. The women were dressed in bright colored dresses and head wraps, and the men in their finest dashikis and bubus.

When the King gave the signal the drummers began to play and the singers began to sing and each man lined up and took their calabashes and poured their wine into the royal wine pot in the center of the village.

Once each man had finished pouring his wine into the royal wine pot the King raised his right arm and there was silence. The King took the royal cup that only his lips could touch and dipped it into the royal wine pot. He raised his

—

cup to heaven with both hands and made a blessing: "Long life and health to the beautiful men, women and children in my village. May the Creator of the Heavens and the Earth always remember you and your loved ones!"

Then the King took a sip of the palm wine from the royal cup. The King rolled the palm wine around in his mouth and made a face. The King turned and spat the palm wine out! He took another cup full of palm wine from the royal wine pot, swished that around in his mouth and then spat that out also. "Water! This is water!

You see just like Ayo all of the other men in the village had the same idea. None of the men wanted to give away their palm wine at a free party!

Now all of that means this: What you put into a thing is exactly what you will get out!

BRUH RABBIT AND BRUH TURTLE

A lot of people don't know this but once upon a time Bruh Rabbit had a long, fluffy white tail. His tail was just as long as Bruh Fox's and Bruh Dog's.

Bruh Rabbit was very proud of his long, fluffy tail. He would always be brushing it and swishing it around. Bruh Rabbit was so good with that tail that he could knock flies out of the air with it!

This is the story of how Bruh Rabbit lost his long, fluffy white tail.

It was early one Saturday morning and Bruh Rabbit was on the bank of a wide but shallow river. Bruh Rabbit was talking to Bruh Turtle who was wading in the water next to the shore. Bruh Rabbit was eating the "sweetgrass" that grew on the banks of that wide but shallow river.

Bruh Rabbit had two paws full of "sweetgrass" and he would eat a little, and then he would talk a little; he would eat a little and then he would talk a little, and before long

Bruh Rabbit looked around and he had eaten up all of the "sweetgrass" on the bank of the river.

Well Bruh Rabbit really liked to eat and he was not even close to being full! He said to himself, "What am I going to do now that I have eaten all of the "sweetgrass.....?" and as he looked across that wide but shallow river he saw "sweetgrass" as far as the eyes could see.

But there was a problem: Bruh Rabbit hated water and he couldn't swim! But Bruh Rabbit was smart and (snap) just like that he came up with a plan!

Bruh Rabbit said to Bruh Turtle, "Bruh Turtle, me and my cousin was just talking the other day. Now my cousin said that when you add up all of the Rabbit aunts and uncles, and first cousins and second cousins twice removed the Rabbit family has the biggest family in this here county. But I told him "No! No! No!" I told him when you add up the Turtle aunts and uncles and first cousins and second cousins twice removed the Turtles have the biggest family in this here county!"

"But Bruh Turtle my cousin is from Missouri and he told me that I have to show him the facts! I am going to be meeting with him next week and when I meet with him I want to be able to tell him exactly how many turtles there are in this here county! So if it is not a big problem could you have the rest of your family come to this river so that I can count them and be able to tell my cousin just how many Turtles there are in this here county next week?!"

Bruh Turtle said, "Why sure Bruh Rabbit, I can do that!" Now Bruh Turtle was a little slow but he thought it was nice of Bruh Rabbit to be talking good about him behind his back!

One hour later that wide but shallow river was full of Bruh Turtle's kin-people.

Bruh Rabbit started to count the Turtles: "One. Two. Three. Four. Five….." Then Bruh Rabbit called Bruh Turtle to him and said, "Bruh Turtle. I'm having a little bit of a problem here. All of your aunts and uncles and first cousins and second cousins twice removed look alike, and they keep moving around, and I can't keep track if I have counted them or not."

"This is what I need you to do: have your kin-people form one straight line across the river. Then I will be able to count each one. To make sure I don't count any Turtle twice I will step on their backonce I've counted them!"

Well Bruh Turtle thought that this was a great idea so he had his kin-people form a line across that wide but shallow river. Bruh Rabbit stepped on the first Turtle's back. "One," he said. He stepped on the second Turtle's back. "Two," he said. He stepped on the third and fourth and fifth and sixth Turtle's back and before he counted to thirty Bruh Rabbit had crossed that wide but shallow river without getting a drop of water on him!

The minute Bruh Rabbit had crossed that river he was so greedy that he began to grab pawfuls of "sweetgrass" and gobble them down!

Bruh Turtle slowly crossed the river and said to Bruh Rabbit, "Bruh Rabbit. Bruh Rabbit! You haven't finished counting all of my kin-people yet!"

Bruh Rabbit looked Bruh Turtle straight in the eye and laughed! "Bruh Turtle I could care less how many Turtles there are in this here county. All I wanted to do was to get over on this side of the river so that I could get me some more of this "sweetgrass!" So excuse me so I can get back to eating!" Bruh Rabbit laughed and turned his back on Bruh Turtle and began to eat more "sweetgrass."

Well as you can imagine this made Bruh Turtle kind of angry to have been fooled like he had been. As Bruh Rabbit was eating that "sweetgrass" Bruh Turtle quietly snuck up behind him and "Snap!" Bruh Turtle bit Bruh Rabbit's long fluffy white tail off!

Bruh Rabbit jumped up in the air and when he landed he hopped as quick as he could into the forest....without his long fluffy white tail.

Now from that day to this day Turtles and Rabbits don't get along and all the Rabbits that you see have short stubby tails because early one Saturday morning Bruh Rabbit tricked Bruh Turtle to get across that wide but shallow river!

WHEN THE DEVIL
GETS HIS HANDS ON YOU...

It was way back in the Creation Days and it was early on that first Friday morning. God and his right-hand man, Michael, the archangel, were sitting and they were looking out over Creation.

Well Michael looked and God looked and they noticed that the waters were empty. God said to Michael, "You know Michael, I think I will make me some fishes."

Michael said, "God, what is a fish?" See this was that First Friday morning during Creation Days and Michael had never seen a fish...

God said, "Watch!" And God thought "Bass" and bass be! God thought "Salmon" and salmon be! God thought "Perch" and perch be! God thought "Haddock" and haddock be! But of all the fish God thought that first Friday morning the one he was most proud of was his "Catfish."

The reason God was so proud of his catfish was because it was the prettiest fish God created that day.

God made some catfish with beautiful blue shiny scales. Other catfish he made with glorious gold shiny scales. And still other catfish God gave radiant red shiny scales.

When those catfish would come up near the surface of the water and the sunlight would come down and hit them it was like diamonds swimming through the water!

Well God created a whole lot of fish that morning to the point that the waters were teeming with fish. The fish were so packed in the waters that they were one on top of another and some started jumping out of the water just to get some relief!

God turned to Michael and said, "Well, we have us another problem now: a fish overpopulation problem!" God told Michael to follow him up to the Big House so that they could discuss it over lunch.

On the way up to the Big House God said to Michael, "Well Michael, I've been thinking.

Should we give birds fur or should we give birds feathers?" But that is another story!

Well it was around about 5pm that same first Friday and here he comes walking down the road. And he just knew he was "Clean! Clean! Clean!" Talking about the Devil!

The Devil had on a bright orange Fedora hat with that wide brim…and he had it pushed way on the back of his head! He had on a two-piece lemon-lime green polyester suit with bell bottom pants! He had on a white and pink, polka dot tie, no shirt and no shoes. And he just knew that he was "Looking good! Looking good! Looking good!"

You know it wasn't around 5pm, it was closer to 5:30pm because the Devil had gotten off of work at 5pm, he had gotten paid and then went to the store to buy the suit he had on!

Well the Devil was walking by the pond and he looked over and he saw those beautiful blue, glorious gold and radiant red catfish in the water. The Devil said to himself, "It these are the prettiest looking fish in the sea I'll bet they are the best "tastinest" fish in the sea!"

So the Devil rolled up the bell bottom pants he had on and he:

"Waded in the water'
Waded in the water children
Waded in the water.
God done troubled the water!"

The Devil grabbed a handful of those catfish and he started throwing them up on the bank. Those catfish started popping and flopping around (kind of like fish out of water)!

So the Devil came back up out of the water and made himself some coleslaw, he put some potato salad on ice, he built himself a fire and put a pot of grease on. As that grease was getting hot the Devil made preparations for the world's first fish fry! It was a Friday night right?!

The Devil grabbed each one of those catfish that he had thrown up on the bank of the water and he began to scrape all of those beautiful shiny scales off of them. Even after the catfish that had had their scales taken off were set aside (while the grease was getting hot) they still popped and flopped around!

The Devil was just getting ready to take those catfish and put them in that nice hot grease when he looked up...and who did he see? God himself!

God looked at his beautiful catfish that the Devil had taken the scales off of and said, "Devil! Devil! What have you done to my beautiful catfish?!"

The Devil was feeling angry for getting caught before he had a chance to taste those catfish and he replied (under his breath), "Well God, you know everything. Why don't you tell me what I've done!?"

But then the Devil saw those thunderbolts and lightning in God's eyes and he changed his tune.

The Devil said, "Well God, I was walking down the road and I looked over and saw all of those catfish in the water...all piled one on the other. So I said to myself that if I take some of the catfish out of the water that will make more room for the others....!"

God looked the Devil straight in the eyes and said, "You are a liar, and the truth ain't in you! Put my catfish back in my water!"

The Devil took those catfish on the bank and threw them back into the water. The second those catfish felt the cold water they began to feel pain all over their body where they had lost their scales. They all went down to the bottom of the pond and began to roll in the black mud to try to ease their pain.....

Well, time come and time go. The soreness went away from the catfish but their scales never grew back. So from that day to this day when you see a catfish they still have those long whiskers but you won't find one scale on a catfish's body...all because of when the Devil got his hands on those first catfish....

But that is only half of the story. The other half of the story is: remember when the Devil waded in the water and threw those catfish up on to the bank? What did those catfish do? They flopped around like fish out of water right? And even after the Devil had scaled the catfish and scraped off their beautiful scales they still were popping and flopping around. They didn't just lay there and give up.

The truth of the matter is those catfish were struggling, even when things looked the worst and all looked lost!

And the truth is if God will come and see about a catfish when it is in trouble God will come and see about any and all of us when we have troubles if we struggle and don't give up!

AESOP RETOLD

WAMBUI AND THE LION

Once upon a time in the land of the Gikuyu, in the central area of Kenya, Eastern Africa, there lived a young girl named Wambui. Wambui means "singer of songs" in KiSwahili. Wambui was well-named for as soon as she could speak she would create songs to please herself, her playmates, and her parents.

When she was of age Wambui had her irua (rites of passage) and became a young maiden ready for marriage. To celebrate her new status in the mbari (her homestead) Wambui created a new song. Each day Wambui would sing her song on her way to fill her gourds full of streamwater, and on her return to her mbari:

"One day my love will come,
and take me away.
I know he will be the one,
because he will be strong and brave!"

And everyday Wambui would go to the stream and fill her gourds full of streamwater and on her way to the stream and back to her mbari she would sing her song.

One day a young lion, brown, strong, and graceful, was walking through the bush. He heard Wambui's beautiful voice over the other sounds of the bush and stopped. The lion crept up to the edge of the bush near the stream and knelt.

Now the young lion could clearly hear Wambui's words and when he saw Wambui he fell deeply, deeply, *deeply* in love with her. He lay quietly at the edge of the bush, watched Wambui fill her gourds, and listened to her song:

> *"One day my love will come,*
> *and take me away.*
> *I know he will be the one,*
> *because he will be strong and brave!"*

Each day after this the young lion would wait at the edge of the bush for Wambui to appear. And each day the young lion would watch Wambui fill her gourds full of streamwater and listen to the words of her song.

That day Wambui had just finished filling her gourds full of streamwater and was preparing to return to her mbari.

The young lion bounded out of the bush heading straight for Wambui. Wambui shook with fear when she saw the young lion's powerful paws, and claws, and jaws. She realized she could not get away and stood trembling in the path of the lion. The young lion came right up to Wambui and knelt at her feet.

"Maiden, everyday I have listened to your words and heard your beautiful voice and I have fallen deeply in love with you," the young lion purred. "I can tell by your beads, bracelets, and the clothes you are wearing that you are a maiden not yet given for marriage. I must have your hand in marriage," he pleaded.

Wambui replied, "Sir Lion, I am amazed that you know Gikuyu culture well and respect it. You therefore know that you must ask my father for my hand in marriage."

Without even hesitating, without even thinking, the young lion roared, "I agree!"

Together Wambui and the young lion returned to Wambui's mbari.

When the people in the mbari saw the young lion walking with Wambui they all ran into their dwellings in fear. Wambui entered her father's compound and called to him in a plaintive voice: "Baba Mugo! Baba Mugo!"

When Baba Mugo came out of his dwelling and saw the lion's powerful paws, and claws, and jaws he too shook with fear.

The lion strode confidently up to Baba Mugo and spoke. "Sir, I have come to ask for your daughter's hand in marriage. Everyday I have listened to her sing her song and I have fallen deeply in love with her. Tell me what I must do to have her hand in marriage."

Baba Mugo crossed his arms on his chest. Then he placed his right hand on the side of his head. Next Baba Mugo closed his eyes and placed his right hand across his mouth. All the while Baba Mugo was deep in thought as to what his response to the young lion's request should be.

Baba Mugo then replied, "Sir Lion, you have spoken well. I will <u>consider</u> your desire to have Wambui for your wife under one condition. I fear that in your passion you may harm my daughter. Only if you agree to have your claws and teethe removed will I even consider your request for my daughter's hand in marriage."

The young lion did not even hesitate, he did not even think. His love for Wambui was so strong he roared, "I agree!"

Baba Mugo sent for the village herbalist and told him that the young lion had agreed to have his teethe and claws removed.

The herbalist went into the bush and collected the plants and herbs he needed for his magic mixture. He put the plants and herbs in a bowl and pounded them with a rounded stone into a powder. Then the herbalist chanted secret words over the potion.

The herbalist returned to Baba Mugo's compound. He poured the magic powder into the palms of his hands and then blew it into the lion's face.

Suddenly, the lion let out a mighty, painful roar, "*AAaaarroooarr!*"

Then *Pop! Pop! Pop!* Each one of the lion's teethe popped out of his mouth.

Then *Pop! Pop! Pop!* Each one of the lion's claws popped from his paws. Then the lion let out another mighty roar: "*AAaaarroooarr!*"

Toothless and clawless the once powerful young lion turned to Baba Mugo, who stood standing with his arm around his daughter.

"Now sir," the young lion slurred, popping his gums and rubbing his clawless paws, "I have done what you requested. Please grant me Wambui's hand in marriage."

"Foolish creature!" Baba Mugo said sternly, "I have considered your request and my answer is *No!*"

"Look at your useless paws and your useless jaws! Once you were strong and powerful and commanded fear and respect from all who crossed your path. But now you have acted without considering the consequences. You have made yourself unfit to

---

be respected! Without your claws and teethe you are not a lion at all!" Baba Mugo stated.

He whistled loudly: "*Thweeeeeeet!*" and all of the men, women, and even the small children in the mbari came out of their dwellings and gathered in Baba Mugo's compound.

Baba Mugo showed them the lion that was no longer a lion at all and they all began to laugh at the beast, suck their teethe and point their fingers. The young lion was embarrassed but all he could do was whimper. He tucked his tail between his legs and scurried back into the bush.

Wambui cried tears of happiness and hugged her father. She thanked him for protecting her and for his wisdom. As Wambui made her way back to her dwelling she began to sing her song:

> *"One day my love will come,*
> *and take me away.*
> *I know he will be the one,*
> *because he will be strong and brave*
> *................and not FOOLISH!"*

THE COMMUNITY OF MICE

Now some people really like cats, and some people really don't! But I can tell you one people who really don't like cats: the Mouse-people! The Mouse-people really don't like cats because cats like to gobble mice up for dinner (and breakfast and lunch too!)

This story is about a smart little City mouse that came up with a plan that saved his family and the community of mice he lived with. The story takes place a long time ago when mice could do everything you see people doing today. And, as everybody knows, anything can happen in a story!

City mouse loved living in the city. He loved hanging out with the other city mice. He loved going to the corner store and picking up things for his mother. He loved the trash and bottles and cans (the litter) that were everywhere because that meant there was always some food in the trash and something to drink in the bottles and cans that people threw down.

City mouse, his mother and father, his sisters and brothers, all lived in a house with a community of mice. Now also in this house there lived a thin, old lady.

The thin old lady was not the cleanest housekeeper! In fact, after she ate, she left food out on the table for days. And even when she did take her dishes and put them in the kitchen sink she left the dishes in the sink for days!

In the beginning the mice would wait until night time, when the thin old lady had went to bed, before they would come out of their hiding places and eat the food that the thin old lady left on the table and in her sink.

After a while though, when the thin old lady went for her morning walk or went to visit friends, the mice started coming out to eat the food the thin old lady left on her table and in her sink in the middle of the day.

Finally, the mice didn't even wait for the thin old lady to leave the house! The mice would come out of their hiding places in the middle of the day, when the thin old lady was in the house, and eat the food she left out on the table and in her sink.

Sometimes the thin old lady would throw things at the mice but they dodged whatever she threw and kept on eating!

One day City mouse's mother received a letter from her sister who lived in the country.

The letter said that City mouse's cousin, Country mouse, wanted to visit the city. You see, Country mouse had never been to the city and he wanted to see what it was like to live in the city. City mouse happily volunteered to go to the country to get his cousin and bring him to the city.

Now how do you think City mouse got to the country? That's right, he hopped a bus to the country!

When City mouse got to the country he felt sorry for Country mouse and his family. Country mouse and his family lived in an apple orchard. And Country mouse and his family mostly ate apples and roots and berries that they could find from time to time.

And in the apple orchard there wasn't any trash or bottles or cans anywhere. But most of all City mouse didn't like the country because he felt the country was soooooo BORING! There wasn't anything to do and nowhere to go!

But the problem was the next bus back to the city wasn't for 3 days! City mouse couldn't wait to get back to the city, and after three long days he and Country mouse hopped another bus back to the city.

When they finally got back to the city City mouse took Country mouse to hang out with his friends. City mouse took Country mouse to the corner store and showed him all of the things there. City mouse showed Country mouse all of the trash and bottles and cans on the streets.

Country mouse didn't like hanging out with City mouse's friends. Country mouse didn't like the corner store. Country mouse didn't like all of the trash and bottles and cans that were everywhere. But Country mouse really, really didn't like all of the noise in the city! Country mouse was used to the peace and quiet in the country.

Then City mouse took Country mouse to the house where he and his family and the community of mice lived. But something was wrong! All of the mice were afraid to leave their hiding places! Some of the mice were hiding in the attic; some of the mice were hiding behind the walls of the house; and some of the mice were hiding in the basement.

City mouse's mother told him that since City mouse had spent 3 days in the country that the thin old lady had went out and bought herself a Cat!

City mouse's mother said that that Cat was quick, quiet, and smart!

Every-time one of the mice left their hiding place to get the food that the thin old lady left out on the table or in the sink the Cat would chase them and catch them with his paws and gobble them up! City mouse's mother said that once the Cat began to chase a mouse he <u>always</u> caught the mouse with his paws and gobbled him up!

When Country mouse heard that there was a Cat in the house he begged City mouse to take him back to the country! Country mouse told City mouse that he would rather live safe in the country with a little food than live in fear with a lot of food in the city! Country mouse wanted to go home!

Well, the very next morning City mouse and Country mouse hopped a bus back to the country. And just like before City mouse had to wait another three days before he could hop a bus back to the city!

When City mouse got back to the city things had gone from bad to worse at his house! The quick, and quiet, and smart Cat had gobbled up ten more mice in the three days he had been gone.

Mayor Mouse decided to call a big meeting of the community of mice to see what could be done about the Cat. Mayor Mouse made a long speech that almost put everybody to sleep, but at the end of the speech he asked if any of the mice had a solution to the Cat gobbling up the mice. Everybody was silent.

Then one of the mice said, "I have an idea." "Yes," said Mayor Mouse. "Well, why don't we put a bell around the Cat's neck! That way whenever he's around we will hear the bell and he won't be able to sneak up on any of us!"

All of the mice cheered at this idea because it would solve their problem. Then Mayor Mouse responded, "I have just one question: Who will put the bell around the Cat's neck?" All of the mice became quiet then. You see, sometimes a great idea is not such a great idea because it is impossible to do!

Everybody was quiet until smart little City mouse spoke up. "I have an idea," City mouse said. "Yes," replied Mayor Mouse.

"First," City mouse began, "we gather up all of the food we can and store it away." "Yes, and then what?" asked Mayor Mouse. "And then nothing," replied City mouse.

———

Then City mouse explained the rest of his plan to the mice. The community of mice agreed to work together to make the plan successful.

The very next morning the thin old lady saw a sight that made her heart jump with joy! When she was leaving her house to take her morning walk she saw all of the community of mice leaving her house and going into the abandoned building next to her house.

When she returned home later that morning she did not see or hear a single mouse in her house. Two days, then three, four, five, six and a whole week went by and no mice. Two weeks, then three weeks, and then a whole month went by and the thin old lady didn't see or hear any mice. Good, thought the thin old lady, no more mice for me!

Well, like I said earlier some people really, really like cats and some people really, really don't like cats. The thin old lady really, really _didn't_ like cats but she had bought one to get rid of the mice.

Now that the mice were gone the thin old lady began to remember why she really, really didn't like cats: she didn't like cleaning the cat litter box, she didn't like that the cat scratched up her furniture with its claws, she didn't like that the cat left cat hairs all over her furniture, and now that there weren't any mice, she didn't like spending her money to buy cat food for the Cat.

The thin old lady called her sister who lived on the other-side of the city (and who really, really _did_ like cats) and asked her did she want another cat. Yes, of course, her sister said, bring me that beautiful cat right away!

And that is exactly what the thin old lady did. She put her cat in a carrying case and hopped a bus and took her sister her cat.

That night the thin old lady went to bed happy because she had gotten rid of her cat and all of the mice in her house.

And the very same night that the thin old lady took her cat to her sister's house the community of mice came from their hiding places and ate the food the thin old lady left on her table, and the food the thin old lady left in the sink........and each one always remembered to be as quiet as a mouse.

THE PARTS OF THE BODY

Once upon a time a Man went for a walk in the country. Once he got to an apple orchard he realized how tired he was and decided to take a nap at the foot of an apple tree. When he was fast asleep some of the parts of his body began to argue about who was the most important part of his body.

The _eyes_ said that they were the most important part of the body because if they didn't see the food the body would starve.

The _hands_ said no, they were the most important part of the body because if they didn't pick the food the body would starve.

The _mouth_ said no, no! If it didn't chew the food the body would starve.

The _throat_ said no, no, no! It was the most important part of the body because if it didn't swallow the food the body would starve.

Then the _stomach_ said no, no, no, no!. If it didn't digest the food the body would starve.

All of the parts of the body argued and argued telling each other that they were the most important part of the body until each one became angry with other parts and decided that it would not cooperate (work) with the other parts of the body.

Finally, the Man's brain spoke up. The brain explained that unless all the parts of the body worked together the body would not be strong and healthy. In fact, if the parts of the body didn't cooperate with each other and work together, the body would get weaker and weaker and the body might get sick and die. But, the brain said, if the parts cooperated with one another the body would be healthy and live. This made sense to the parts of the Man's body, and they all agreed to work together.

When the Man woke up from his nap he stretched and yawn, and looking up, he saw the apple tree, full of red apples. With his hands he plucked the juiciest apple from the tree that his eyes saw. He bit the apple with his mouth and began to chew the apple into tiny little pieces. Then he swallowed the apple pieces with his throat down into the stomach.

Then the stomach began to digest the apple so that the whole body could get strong and healthy.

And from that day to this day the Man's brain, and eyes, and hands, and mouth, and throat, and stomach have worked together, and the Man and his body lived happily ever after.

MR. GRASSHOPPER
AND THE ANTS

One bright, summer sunshiny day Mr. Grasshopper decided to visit the village of the Ants.

When he got there he found out that all those Ants wanted to do was:

"Work! Work! Work! Work! Work Work! Work! Work! Work! Work! Work! Work! Work! Work!"

Mr. Grasshopper didn't like to do a whole lot of work. Mr. Grasshopper liked to sing, and he liked to dance. All Summer long Mr. Grasshopper tried to teach those Ants his favorite song and his favorite dance, but they wouldn't listen. But now you can learn Mr. Grasshopper's favorite dance and song.

This is Mr. Grasshopper's favorite dance:

1. *Right hand up and left foot step back.*
2. *Left foot even with right foot and clap.*
3. *Left hand up and right foot step back.*
4. *Right foot even with left foot and clap.*

As Mr. Grasshopper would do his favorite dance he would sing his favorite song:

"If you will give me a chance,
I'll teach you to sing and dance!"
"If you will give me a chance,
I'll teach you to sing and dance!"

Let's try Mr. Grasshopper's favorite song and dance right now!

All Summer long Mr. Grasshopper tried to teach those Ants his favorite song and dance but they wouldn't listen. All they wanted to do was:

"Work! Work! Work! Work! Work Work! Work!
Work! Work! Work! Work! Work! Work! Work!"

Fix up their houses
and put away food for the Winter!
Fix up their houses
and put away food for the Winter!

As everyone knows after the Summer comes the Fall. Beautiful red and orange and brown and yellow leaves had fallen to the ground. And Mr. Grasshopper was still visiting the village of the Ants and he was still trying to teach them his favorite song and his favorite dance. Do you remember how they go?

Let's try Mr. Grasshopper's favorite song and dance right now!

But except for a couple of the children Ants none of those Ants would even listen to Mr. Grasshopper. All they wanted to do was:

"Work! Work! Work! Work! Work Work! Work! Work! Work! Work! Work! Work! Work! Work!"

Fix up their houses
and put away food for the Winter!
Fix up their houses
and put away food for the Winter!

After the Fall season comes the Winter. In the Wintertime it is cold and icy. All of those Ants went into their nice, warm homes and ate the food they had stored up over the Summer and Fall.

But Mr. Grasshopper didn't have a home to go to. All Summer and all Fall he had slept outside because it was warm. And Mr. Grasshopper didn't have any food because he had eaten the free food-the leaves and grass- all Summer and all Fall.

So Mr. Grasshopper decided that he would see if he could stay with one of the Ants in the village. Mr. Grasshopper went to each Ant house, knocked on the door and said: *"Can I come inside? I'm cold. Can I have something to eat? I'm hungry!"*

Each one of those Ants asked Mr. Grasshopper why he didn't have any food or a home to live in? He told them that he had been singing and dancing all Summer and Fall. Each Ant told Mr. Grasshopper to go and sing and dance now to keep himself warm! Then they slammed the door in his face.

Mr. Grasshopper was so cold that he thought he was going to freeze! Mr. Grasshopper was so hungry that he thought he was going to starve!

Mr. Grasshopper was getting ready to leave the village of the Ants when he saw one last Ant house that he hadn't tried. He crawled through the ice and snow. Mr. Grasshopper knocked on the door and was shivering when the Daddy Ant opened the door. He said: *"Can I come inside? I'm cold. Can I have something to eat? I'm hungry!"*

The Daddy Ant was getting ready to slam the door closed in Mr. Grasshopper's face when one of the children Ants said, *"Daddy! That's Mr. Grasshopper! All Summer and all Fall he taught us how to sing! He taught us how to dance! And he taught us how to have fun!"*

That gave the Daddy Ant an idea. He said to Mr. Grasshopper: "You know how cold and boring the Winter can be in our village. What if you stayed with my family for the rest of the Winter (until next Spring) and you can eat what we eat, and in exchange you can teach my children all of your songs and all of your dances?"

Mr. Grasshopper jumped for joy and said, *"Yes!"* Then he said, *"My first lesson starts right now! Let's do my favorite song and my favorite dance! One, two, three, four:*

"If you will give me a chance,
I'll teach you to sing and dance!"
"If you will give me a chance,
I'll teach you to sing and dance!"

———
135

AFTERWORDS

The **Retold Stories** in this book came from various sources. I am usually entertained by most stories but some inspire me to tell them myself....

"The Wrestling Match" was inspired by the story, "The Wrestling Match of the Two Buddhas," from "The Magic Listening Cap: More Folk Tales from Japan" retold and illustrated by Yoshiko Uchida (Creative Arts Book Company, 1987)

"The Man and the Woman" was inspired by "The Man Makes and the Woman Takes," "When the Devil Touches You" by "The Devil's Doing," and "Snake and Hunter" by "The Trouble with Helping Out" all from "African American Folktales: Stories from Black Traditions in the New World selected and edited by Roger D. Abrahams (Pantheon Books 1985)

"The Big Wind" is a retelling of "The Big Wind" from "The Days When the Animals Talked" by William J. Faulkner (Africa World Press 1993)

"Bruh Rabbit and Bruh Turtle" and "Ayo and the Palm Wine" were developed after hearing versions of them performed by unknown storytellers.

The **Aesop Retold** stories were inspired by the Aesop fables "Grasshopper and the Ants," "Lion in Love," "Country Mouse and City Mouse," "Belling the Cat," and "The Belly and the Members."

NOTES

NOTES